Banners with a Conscience

37 Banners on Sensitive Subjects

Dale A. Bargmann

CPH
SAINT LOUIS

To Jim and Jennie and my friends
at Our Father Lutheran Church

All Scripture quotations, unless otherwise indicated, are taken from the HOLY BIBLE, NEW INTERNATIONAL VERSION®. NIV®. Copyright © 1973, 1978, 1984 by International Bible Society. Used by permission of Zondervan Publishing House. All rights reserved.

Scripture quotations marked KJV are from the King James or Authorized Version of the Bible.

Scripture quotations marked RSV are from the Revised Standard Version of the Bible, copyrighted 1946, 1952, © 1971, 1973 by the Division of Christian Education of the National Council of the Churches of Christ in the U.S.A., and are used by permission.

Copyright © 1997 Concordia Publishing House
3558 S. Jefferson Avenue, St. Louis, MO 63118-3968
Manufactured in the United States of America.

Library of Congress Cataloging-in-Publication Data

Bargmann, Dale, 1947-
        Banners with conscience : 37 banners on sensitive issues / Dale A. Bargmann.
        p.   cm.
        ISBN 0-570-04897-4
        1. Church pennants.   I. Title.
    BV168.F5B34   1997
    246' .55—DC20   96-28453

1   2   3   4   5   6   7   8   9   10   06   05   04   03   02   01   00   99   98   97

Contents

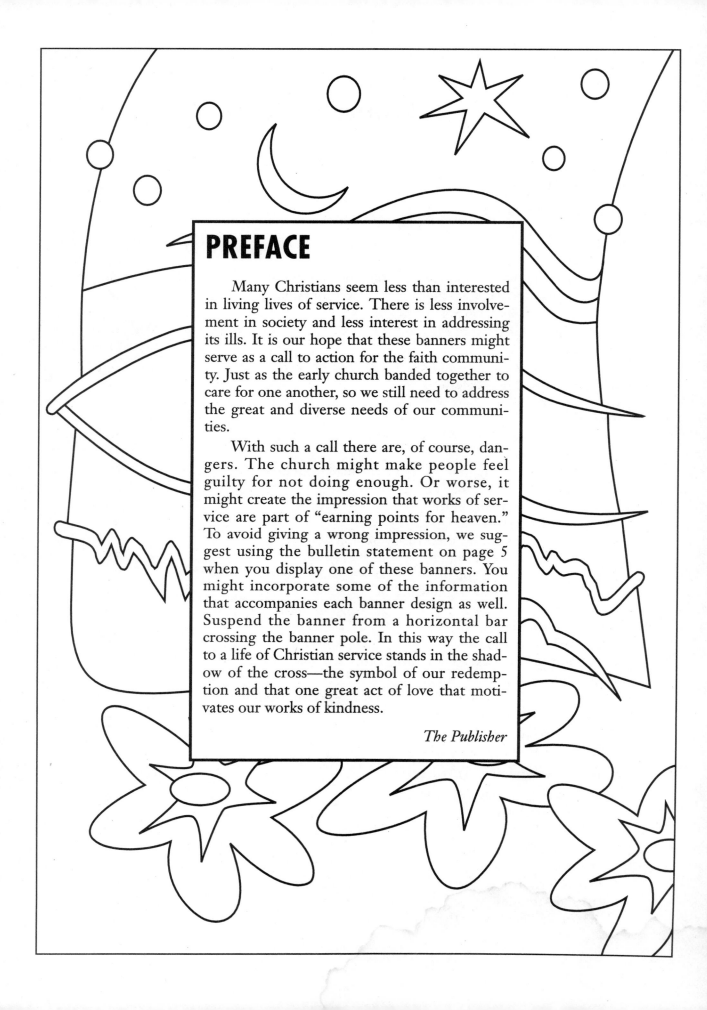

PREFACE

Many Christians seem less than interested in living lives of service. There is less involvement in society and less interest in addressing its ills. It is our hope that these banners might serve as a call to action for the faith community. Just as the early church banded together to care for one another, so we still need to address the great and diverse needs of our communities.

With such a call there are, of course, dangers. The church might make people feel guilty for not doing enough. Or worse, it might create the impression that works of service are part of "earning points for heaven." To avoid giving a wrong impression, we suggest using the bulletin statement on page 5 when you display one of these banners. You might incorporate some of the information that accompanies each banner design as well. Suspend the banner from a horizontal bar crossing the banner pole. In this way the call to a life of Christian service stands in the shadow of the cross—the symbol of our redemption and that one great act of love that motivates our works of kindness.

The Publisher

BULLETIN STATEMENT— BECAUSE HE FIRST LOVED US

Our human care banner reminds us of the many needs in society. With so much to do, how does the Christian respond?

First, there are many organizations that address the larger concerns: hunger, poverty, children in need. These need our donations of money, time, and talents. But there also is much we can do as individuals, as families, and as faith communities.

Why do these things? It's not to gain points for heaven. Our salvation already is assured through the redeeming death and resurrection of Jesus Christ. Neither is our motivation one of moralism—that we *should* or *must* do these things because of faith.

The Christian life of service flows from our faith and our thankfulness for all God has done and continues to do for us. Yes, we know that we are our brother's (and sister's) keeper (Genesis 4:9), but works of love are a fruit of the Spirit and part of the freedom we have in Christ. We cannot be justified by doing good works. Ultimately, "the only thing that counts is faith expressing itself through love" (Galatians 5:6). It is how we "carry each other's burdens" (Galatians 6:2).

Finally, we don't seek recognition for ourselves. Instead, we pray that our kindness will be a witness to others so others will come to know the great love of Jesus through the actions of His followers.

>>> Always preach the Gospel. If necessary, use words. (St. Francis of Assisi)

INTRODUCTION

From ancient times, banners have been used as signals in battle to rally troops and herald the arrival of monarchs or generals. Old Testament references to banners attest to their significance in the history of God's chosen people. The earliest reference, Exodus 17:15, states that "Moses built an altar [to commemorate the Israelite victory over the Amalekites] and called it The LORD is my Banner." Centuries later, Isaiah announced in reference to the coming Messiah: "In that day the Root of Jesse will stand as a banner for the peoples; the nations will rally to Him and His place of rest will be glorious. ... He will raise a banner for the nations and gather the exiles of Israel" (Isaiah 11:10, 12). Through the prophet Jeremiah, God spoke concerning Babylon and the land of the Chaldeans: "Announce and proclaim among the nations, lift up a banner and proclaim it; keep nothing back, but say, 'Babylon will be captured; Bel will be put to shame' " (Jeremiah 50:2). And God comforts us with this image: "He has taken me to the banquet hall, and His banner over me is love" (Song of Songs 2:4).

Clearly, in Old Testament times banners were more than mere decorative cloth hangings. They inspired people, marked the culmination of events, and, most important, signified the presence of God.

Today, banners are displayed outside homes and along main streets, adding beauty to a world of asphalt and brick. In places of worship, they mark the seasons of the liturgical year, raise hymns of praise, and create an atmosphere conducive to worship. But do we use banners to their full potential? Do they provoke thought? Do they focus our attention on the concerns of a troubled world in need of reconciliation? Do they call us to action and move us to share with those around us the message of God's grace, which leads to healing and restoration?

The designs on the following pages reflect the concerns of everyday life. Daily, our senses are bombarded by news stories of children accidentally shot while playing with supposedly unloaded guns purchased by parents for protection against neighborhood violence. We hear of young people killed while playing outside their homes, the victims of gang initiation rites. We watch live reports of fire bombings or newborn infants found in Dumpsters and wonder why life has become so disposable. There are reports of large corporations announcing new rounds of layoffs. Tabloids and magazines barrage us with articles on AIDS/HIV, drugs, weight-loss plans, divorce, infidelity, custody battles, the homeless, natural and man-made disasters, grieving families, war … It's overwhelming.

But the sun rises every day to offer another opportunity for service. As pinks, oranges,

reds, blues, and greens paint the sky, we can read in the Bible: "People brought to Him all who were ill with various diseases, those suffering severe pain, the demon-possessed, those having seizures, and the paralyzed, and He healed them" (Matthew 4:24). Jesus did not avoid those in need of healing and comfort. He knew that actions spoke louder than words to the leper or to those suffering from prolonged illness. He fed the multitudes. By His actions, He revealed the message of the Gospel.

Jesus' ministry is an example of how we are to bring the Gospel to a needy world. Words alone cannot express the message of salvation to those numbed by misfortune and tragedy. These banners depict some of today's most important, even most controversial, issues. Inspired by traditional sources such as the Bible and hymns—as well as magazine articles, news stories, and personal observation—these designs, I hope, will provoke thought, discussion, and action. Now, more than ever, the world needs to hear Jesus' message of healing, reconciliation, and love.

GATHERING NECESSARY ITEMS

Design Notebook: It is a good idea to have a loose-leaf binder with filler paper handy at all times. You can keep procedural notes, lists of supplies, fabric swatches, color ideas, and copies of banner designs in your notebook for easier reference.

CONSTRUCTION TOOLS AND MATERIALS

Most of the tools and materials needed for constructing the designs in this book are listed below. They are not all necessary for any one design. At the beginning of a banner project, check the instructions first before deciding what to buy. (Most of these supplies can be obtained through craft, art, drafting, cloth or hardware stores.)

Cutting tools

- Scissors—two pairs: one for paper, one reserved for cloth (paper dulls cutting edges)
- X-Acto knife and blades

Marking tools

- No. 2 pencils or .7 mm automatic pencils with HB black leads
- Medium ballpoint pens—black and blue
- Eagle Prismapastel pencils or Crayola colored pencils in light and dark colors for marking fabric
- Wooden stick (¾" × ¾" × 3') to serve as a makeshift compass for drawing large circles and arcs. For a pivot, drill a ¼" hole near one end and insert a pencil, eraser end

down. Use a small C-clamp to secure another pencil, point down, to the other end. The C-clamp allows for adjustment to any radius.
- Circle templates, small compass, or French curves—aids for drawing curves and circles.

Paper for patterns

- Tissue gift-wrapping paper (similar in weight to that used for dressmakers' patterns)
- Butcher paper
- Brown wrapping paper
- Newspaper, especially the classified ads
- Wide rolls of wrapping paper, particularly those with the pattern printed only on one side

Bonding materials

- Scotch brand transparent tape (green package)
- Scotch brand removable tape (blue package) or Scotch Safe-Release brand masking tape.
- Double-stick tape
- Masking tape
- Elmer's Glue-All brand general-purpose white glue (works best with cotton and cotton blends)
- Sobo brand glue by Delta or Aleene's brand tacky glue (white craft glues suitable for fabrics)
- Pellon Wonder-Under, Aleene's Ultra Hold Fusible Web, and Therm O Web HeatnBond brands iron-on adhesives with paper backing; 17" wide
- Stitch Witchery brand ¾" wide iron-on bonding web for linings and hems
- Dritz Fray Check brand anti-fraying agent

- Glue sticks
- Velcro strips and adhesive or self-adhesive Velcro.

Miscellaneous

- Plastic fishing tackle box for storing tools and small supplies
- Opaque projector or overhead transparency projector
- Ball-head straight pins
- Lightweight pressing cloth for protecting fabrics from direct contact with the iron (a piece of 100 percent cotton muslin, a cotton dish towel, or an old bedsheet works well)
- L-shaped carpenter's square (18″ and 24″ sides) or a large T-square
- Yardstick
- 12′ retractable tape measure
- 12″ ruler, preferably clear plastic
- Iron and ironing board
- Sewing machine and sewing needle with a selection of thread in colors to match fabrics being used
- Wright's brand bias tape, double or single fold—for finishing raw fabric edges
- Inexpensive paintbrushes, ½″ and 1½″

Hanging supplies

- Hammer, screwdriver, and pliers
- Drill, electric or push type, with bits
- 4d smooth box nails or similar
- S- or 8-hooks (so named because of their shape)
- ¾″ dowels—lengths as needed
- Lock seam or adjustable spring-pressure curtain rods
- Drapery weights
- Fishing line, 15 lb. test or higher

Special purpose materials

- *For outlining*—Crayola or Kodak washable markers; permanent felt-tip markers (regular tip, in black and other colors as needed); fluorescent highlighters; yarn (4-ply,

100 percent acrylic); embroidery paints (preferably the puff type in various colors)
- Spray paint (12 oz. can) or a can of quick-drying enamel, preferably red

Fabric Choices

Pick a fabric supplier with a large selection. There are many attractive fabrics suitable for making banners, but some types work better than others. Generally speaking, 100 percent cottons and cotton blends work best. Avoid stretchy knits (especially 100 percent polyesters) and those with loose weaves or heavy textures.

Recommended fabrics

Broadcloth—100 percent cotton or polyester-cotton blend; 45″ wide; relatively inexpensive; excellent color range, but lighter shades do not cover as well as darker ones.

Cotton sheeting—100 percent cotton; 60″ wide; heavier than broadcloth; covers well.

Felt—100 percent acrylic or polyester; 72″ wide; smooth surface; good color range and intensity; good as a background material; economical, readily available, nonfraying, and does not require lining (although lining does add stability).

Flannel—100 percent cotton (avoid polyester); 45″ wide; limited number of solid colors available; easy to glue; accepts paint well.

Interlock knits—polyester-cotton or polyester-rayon blend; 60″ wide; nonfraying; good color range.

Muslin—100 percent cotton; 45″–108″ wide; primarily available in white and natural unbleached, but also in a number of solid colors; light in weight with a smooth finish; covers well and works well with paints and markers.

Polished Apple brand solids—Polyester-cotton blend; 45″ wide; covers well; good color range with slight sheen.

Poplin—Cotton-polyester blend; 45″ wide; heavier and more opaque than broadcloth; good for backgrounds if lined.

Robe velour—60″ wide; 80 percent acetate/20 percent nylon; gives a plush look similar to velvet but without the weight; non-fraying; good for background; also good for lettering on selected designs.

Trigger cloth—60″ wide; available only in black, white, and basic colors; a good background material on selected designs because of its weight and smooth texture; needs to be lined.

>>> Check sale tables for remnants and misdyed lots. Do not be afraid to mix materials. Plan to use heavier fabrics (felt, poplin, Trigger cloth) for backgrounds and lighter fabrics (flannel, broadcloth) for design elements. Also try drapery and upholstery fabrics for backgrounds, but avoid those with heavy or rough textures or all-over patterns.

Specialty fabrics

Lycra—60 percent Lycra/40 percent nylon; relatively expensive; available in several good bright colors, including fluorescents.

Solid taffeta—100 percent polyester; 60″ wide; good for processional banners.

Lining materials

Drapery lining—48″ wide; polyester-cotton blend.

Fusible interfacing—22″ and 45″ widths.

>>> Sale and remnant tables are a good source of heavy fabrics to use for linings. Extra-wide drapery and upholstery materials, suitable for backing large banners, often can be found at reduced prices as well.

FULL-SIZE DESIGNS

Enlarging the design

Pattern Method

The best way to enlarge designs is to use an opaque projector. This allows the image to be cast directly from the page in the book. Next best is to use an overhead transparency projector, most likely available from the church office. Its biggest advantage is that the design can be scaled to a size that fits the dimensions of the display area. To use an overhead projector, first photocopy the design in the book onto a clear acetate sheet.

1. Project the design onto a smooth wall at eye level. Adjust the image to the desired size by moving the projector toward or away from the wall, measuring with a 12′ tape measure. Then turn the projector off.

2. Prepare the sheet of paper that will serve as the full-size pattern by cutting it to the exact size of the finished banner. Make sure all sides are square. This is an important step if the finished banner is to hang properly because the pattern will be used both for cutting the design pieces and for sizing the background.

3. Turn on the projector and tape the blank pattern paper to the wall within the image area. Use removable tape to prevent wall damage. *Make sure the image is square with the paper.*

4. Trace the design lines in pencil (a marker can bleed through the paper) taking special care with the lettering. Keep a ruler handy for straight lines and a compass, French curve, or circle template for curves.

5. Block the projected image in sections to check for missed lines. Look carefully at the lettering to make sure the lines are plumb with each other.

6. Turn off the projector. Before removing the pattern from the wall, do a final check for any untraced elements.

7. To aid reassembly after cutting, number each shape and indicate its color. Transfer the numbers to the corresponding shapes on the original in the book. Also, to prevent pieces from accidentally being placed upside down, indicate the top of each with a *T.*

8. Set the pattern aside. Do not cut it apart yet. It needs to be kept whole for some of the next steps.

>>> Have a second sheet of paper handy because some of the designs have overlapping design elements that require separate tracings.

....

>>> If projection transparencies are unavailable, make two copies of the chosen design on plain paper. Carefully cut out the design elements, and with double-stick tape, attach them to the glass bed of the projector. Proceed as above, except now you will be tracing the shadows of the shapes.

....

No-Pattern Method

For simple designs with few overlapping elements, consider projecting the design directly onto the cloth pieces, skipping the paper pattern altogether.

1. Project the design directly onto a wall.
2. Use a 12′ tape measure to size the image to the exact size of the finished banner.
3. Attach the cloth pieces to the wall over the image area with Scotch Safe-Release masking tape.
4. Trace the design areas onto the fabrics with clearly contrasting pastel pencils or colored pencils.
5. Cut out the pieces just inside the pencil lines so the lines won't show on the finished banner.

Estimating fabric needs

Background—To determine the amount of background material needed, start with the dimensions of the finished banner. Then

- add 2″ to the *length* to compensate for cutting error, plus 3″ for each hem;
- add 2″ to the *width* to compensate for cutting error, plus 2″ for hems or sewn-in linings (not necessary if lining with fusible interfacing or other materials bonded with Stitch Witchery);
- add another 2″ to both *length* and *width* to compensate for shrinkage from prewashing (not necessary for upholstery fabrics or felt, which do not require preshrinkage); and

- add extra yardage to allow for experimentation with unfamiliar materials and processes.

Lining—Purchase enough material to cover the background plus a little extra.

Fabrics for design elements—Use the full-size pattern to make rough measurements of lettering and color areas. Do not scrimp. Allow for error and experimentation. These measurements also will determine the amount of iron-on adhesive to purchase, if it is being used to attach the design elements to the background.

....

>>> When making estimates, remember that most fabrics, with the exception of those noted previously, are manufactured in 45″ widths.

....

PUTTING THE BANNER TOGETHER

PREPARATIONS

For assembly, it is best to work in a well-lit area on a table large enough to handle the full-size banner. It is also possible to use a carpeted floor or any space where the banner can be left undisturbed until completed.

To prevent puckering and uneven bonding, fabrics (except felt and upholstery materials) must be preshrunk and pressed smooth. Preshrinking is especially important for 100 percent cotton and cotton blends because it removes the sizing or starch that can interfere with bonding. Preshrink the fabrics by putting them through a complete wash and dry cycle. Be sure to check fabric care instructions at the time of purchase. As with regular laundering, light and dark fabrics need to be separated.

Background

Materials

- Carpenter's square or T-square
- 12″ ruler
- Pastel pencils or Crayola colored pencils

(light or dark, to contrast with fabric color)
- Straight pins
- Sharp cloth scissors

Procedure

1. Lay background cloth wrong side up on the work surface and place the carefully squared pattern on top.
2. Align pattern edge with the fabric weave and secure with several straight pins.
3. Use the pattern to measure cutting lines, with allowances for finishing. Add 2½"–3" to the length for each pole loop. Add less to the bottom if using drapery weights. If the lining will be sewn to the back, add 1" to the width for seams. Disregard if the sides will be left as cut edges (as on felt) or if the lining will be bonded to the back.
4. Apply an anti-fraying agent along the cutting lines to prevent edges from unraveling after cutting (unnecessary with felt).

Design pieces

The pattern pieces need to be cut out. Stack them, as work proceeds, according to the color fabric they will be used on later. Set the larger background pieces aside for use as positioning templates during the process of final assembly.

Before tracing the pattern pieces onto their respective fabrics, a method for attaching the fabric design pieces to the background of the banner needs to be determined.

The least expensive method is gluing. White glue is easiest to use with fabrics. Of the ordinary brands on the market, the best is Elmer's Glue-All. It is heavy enough in consistency not to soak in too quickly; its applicator tip delivers a smooth, even flow; and it has demonstrated its capacity to hold banners together, even through years of continuous use.

Also suitable for fabrics, though more expensive, are craft glues such as Sobo glue by Delta and Aleene's tacky glue. All these glues dry clear but have several disadvantages. They can cause moisture-sensitive fabrics to pucker if they aren't first preshrunk; they can bleed through fabrics, leaving a shiny discoloration;

and they do not work well with polyester.

An alternative to gluing is to use highly recommended iron-on adhesives like Pellon Wonder-Under, Aleene's Ultra Hold Fusible Web, or Therm O Web HeatnBond. These can be purchased in prepackaged amounts or off the bolt by the yard. Though somewhat more expensive than gluing, iron-on adhesives provide these advantages to the banner-making process:

- Are easier and faster to use than glue.
- Leave no mess.
- Eliminate frayed edges.
- Can be applied with or against the grain.
- Can be dry cleaned or washed.
- Are good for fabrics that react adversely to moisture.
- Are good with fabrics that do not take glue.

Testing, as always, is the best way to decide on a method. Use 6" swatches of the materials involved. Make one piece a letter like *S* or *E*. Glue pieces of broadcloth, flannel, and poly-cotton sheeting to felt (use Elmer's brand and a craft glue). Then bond the same fabrics with squares of iron-on adhesives following the instructions furnished with the material. Allow the samples to cool and dry completely. Be sure to time the procedures. Compare results.

- Check the edges for fraying and puckering.
- Check for adhesive bleed-through.
- Check to see that the pieces lie flat.
- Check the strength of the bond by trying to pull the pieces apart.

All things considered, the iron-on adhesive usually proves the best. It is more expensive, but this disadvantage seems minor when compared with the time it saves.

ASSEMBLY

To begin

1. Press the background to remove wrinkles.
2. For references, mark seam and hem allowances with straight pins placed parallel to the edges and spaced about 12" apart.

Gluing method

Materials
- Paper pattern pieces
- Fabrics for design pieces
- Straight pins
- Sharp cloth scissors
- Carpenter's square
- Glue

Procedure
1. Lay all fabrics for the design pieces *right side up.* Position pattern pieces on top, also *right side up.* Leave about ¼″ between each piece to be cut. *Align all the letters in the same direction*, that is, on the same grain. Secure all the pattern pieces with straight pins.
2. Cut out pieces using smooth strokes to avoid ragged edges. Check the original design in the book for any abutting elements; if found, cut one piece ¼″ larger than the other so it will fit under the other. Arrange the pieces roughly in position on the background as they are cut.
3. Remove the pins and arrange the pieces in their final position using the reserved pattern templates as guides. Step back to check for reversed letters or awkward spacing.
4. Prepare for gluing. If the design has overlapping elements, the lower elements need to be attached first. Temporarily set the upper ones aside.
5. Working on one element at a time, lay the arm of the carpenter's square across the center of the element. Fold half the element over the carpenter's square, away from the background, and apply a steady, unbroken line of glue along all edges of its underside. Drop it back into position and press down gently. Repeat with the other shapes until half of each is glued. Let them dry thoroughly. Then glue the other halves using the same method.
6. Reposition any pieces that had to be set aside and repeat the gluing procedure.
7. Allow everything to dry completely before handling further.

>>> Do not discard letter patterns. Put them in large clasp envelopes, record the contents of the envelope on the outside, and file the envelope for future projects.

Iron-on adhesive method

Materials
- Fabrics for design pieces
- Iron-on adhesive to cover
- Straight pins
- Sharp cloth scissors
- Iron and ironing board

>>> Read the instructions that come with the iron-on adhesive carefully. Do a test on fabric swatches for each banner.

Procedure
1. Preheat the iron on the dry wool setting (do not use steam).
2. Place the fabric for the design pieces *face down* on the ironing board. Position an adhesive sheet textured side down on top of the fabric.
3. Place the iron on the paper side of the adhesive sheet and press 1–3 seconds *only.* (The object is not to melt the glue but to transfer it to the back of the fabric.) Let cool.
4. Pin paper pattern pieces *right side up* to the front (cloth side) of the prepared fabrics. It is especially important that letters be aligned in the same direction, that is, on the same grain.
5. Cut the design pieces from the prepared fabric according to the pattern. Remove the pins. Carefully peel off the paper backing and position, adhesive side down, on the background. Use the reserved pattern templates as guides.
6. Double-check wording for spelling and reversed or upside-down letters. Also check spacing and alignment.
7. Preheat the iron on dry wool setting.
8. Cover an area with a damp pressing cloth and press approximately 10 seconds. Do not slide the iron back and forth. Lift it to

the next position, overlapping iron placement to ensure complete bonding. *Do not overheat.* (Overheating causes adhesive to migrate back toward the iron.) For large areas, begin fusing in the center and work outward to the sides and corners.

>>> While bonding the design elements, move the banner as little as possible to prevent jostling the arrangement. Place the ironing board adjacent to and level with the work surface and slide the banner onto it for fusing. A sheet of corrugated cardboard also makes a suitable ironing surface if the work surface is the floor or large table. Simply slide the cardboard under the area to be fused.

FINISHING

Lining

Lining is recommended for practically all banners because it gives added stability when hanging. It is optional for banners with backgrounds of felt, but necessary for banners with backgrounds of woven or lightweight fabrics.

Except for felt, upholstery, and drapery fabrics, preshrink lining materials by machine washing or by pressing with an iron and a wet pressing cloth. To prepare iron-on adhesive, dip it in a sink of warm water, lay it flat between bath towels, and pat it dry to remove excess moisture. Hang it to air dry.

Method I—Apply an iron-on adhesive to the back. Primarily for lightweight fabrics, also poplins, linens, wools, and fabrics with special finishes.

1. Trim the banner to its finished size, allowing an extra 3″ at the top for a pole casing. No allowances are needed for the sides or bottom.
2. Place the banner *face side down* on the work surface. Position the adhesive *rough (adhesive) side down* on top of it. Pin it in place along the edges.
3. Preheat the iron on the dry wool setting. Baste at a few points along the edges by pressing lightly with the tip of the iron.

Remove the pins.

4. Cover the adhesive with a damp pressing cloth and fuse about 15 seconds. Do not slide the iron. Fuse section by section, overlapping the previous area. Let cool.
5. Turn the banner over and repeat the ironing process to achieve a secure bond.
6. Trim any excess lining material.

Method II—Bond a heavy fabric to the back. Primarily for felt and heavier background fabrics.

1. Trim the banner to its finished size, allowing 2½″–3″ at the top for a pole casing. No allowances are needed for the sides or bottom.
2. Cut the lining material slightly larger than the banner. Place it *face down* (wrong side up) on the work surface. Position the banner *face up* on top of it.
3. Preheat the iron at the dry wool setting.
4. Place strips of Stitch Witchery between the fabric layers along the edges of the banner.
5. Cover with a damp pressing cloth and press along the edges for 10 seconds. *Do not slide the iron.*
6. Turn the banner over and press along the edges for another 10 seconds.
7. Turn the banner over once more and trim any excess lining material.

>>> With careful handling, the fused edges will not unravel using either of these methods. However, the banners can be dressed up with strips of quilt edging in a color to match the background.

Method III—Stabilize the edges before lining. Primarily for fabrics that unravel easily.

1. Trim the banner to its finished size, allowing 3″ at the top for a pole casing and ¾″ at the bottom and each side.
2. Turn the banner *face down.*
3. Fold the side and bottom edges over, forming ¾″ hems. Press with the iron to crease and bond the hems to the back of the banner with strips of Stitch Witchery.
4. Cut a lining of heavy cloth slightly smaller

than the finished banner and bond it to the background along all the edges with Stitch Witchery.

Method IV—Sew a heavy fabric or drapery lining to the back. An alternate method for felt, medium, and heavyweight fabrics.

1. Trim the banner to its finished size, allowing 3″ at the top for a pole casing and ⅝″ at each side and the bottom.
2. Place the lining material *right side up* on the work surface. Place the banner *face down* on top of it, making sure the grains of the fabrics are aligned.
3. Pin the side and bottom edges together.
4. Set the sewing machine to "straight stretch stitch." Sew the sides and bottom together with a ⅝″ seam, leaving the top end open like a pillow case.
5. Trim the seams and cut the bottom corners off at a 45 degree angle.
6. Turn the banner and lining *right side out*.
7. Sew or bond the top edges together.

Finishing the top edge

The designs in this book work best when hung by inserting a pole through a 3″ casing applied at the top. No matter which lining method has been used, all banners can be finished at the top in the same way.

Procedure

1. Turn the banner *face down*.
2. Mark a line 6″ down from and parallel to the top edge. Fold the top over to meet the line, forming a 3″ casing. Bond with Stitch Witchery.
3. For added security, edge-stitch the casing with a sewing machine set on "straight stretch stitch" or with needle and thread using a simple whipstitch.

>>> All methods provide enough stability so a bottom pole is unnecessary. If the bottom edge should curl or sag, add drapery weights to the lower corners as appropriate.

Outlining design elements

Before any banner is hung, it should be thoughtfully appraised from a distance. If the images fail to stand out or are unclear, simple outlining of one or two design elements can bring them into focus.

Fluorescent highlighters (¼″ wide) add subtle radiance without becoming obtrusive. The best colors are hot pink, yellow, orange, chartreuse, and light blue. Draw lines about 3⁄16″ wide directly on the background or on the edge of the elements. Make samples of both to see which works better.

Permanent felt-tip markers (¼″ tip) in colors contrasting with both the background and the elements being outlined will sharpen definition considerably. For example, outline a white form set against a dark blue background with an orange marker. Or outline a chartreuse form set against a yellow background with a dark green marker. Draw the line ⅛″–¼″ wide on the edge of the forms. This technique works best on 100 percent cottons or cotton blends with a smooth finish.

Yarn (4-ply, 100 percent acrylic) adds a dimension of depth while anchoring the elements in place. The process can be time-consuming, but the results are well worth it. Remember these tips:

• Yarn outlines are best applied after lining.
• Color combinations need to be tested by doing a dry outline first.
• Care should be taken when pressing. (Prolonged exposure to steam can soften the glue and cause the yarn to loosen.)

Procedure

1. Slide a sheet of corrugated cardboard under the area to be outlined.
2. With sharp scissors, cut the end of the yarn square and dab it with glue to prevent unraveling.
3. Outline the shape with an even, unbroken line of white glue about the width of the yarn. Begin at a corner or point, if possible, and lay the yarn gently onto the glue line. Do not pull. Press it in with the fingers.

4. To bend the yarn around corners, secure it with vertical pins stuck down through the strands and into the cardboard.

5. Cut the finishing end of the yarn only after most of the outline is in place.

Fabric paints (puff type) are a good alternative to yarn, especially with fabrics that do not accept glue well. Work quickly to keep the lines uniform. Practice on scraps first. One undesirable quality of fabric paint is its semigloss finish when dry.

Washable marking pens are useful for both outlining and shading. They work well on fabrics that are 100 percent cotton or cotton blends with a smooth finish. Lightly outline the shape with a ¼″–½″ wide line and then, with an inexpensive ½″ watercolor brush, dampen the line and the area immediately around it with tap water. The marker will bleed, creating a subtle color gradation. Allow it to dry naturally. For best results, use colors within the same family as that of the shape being outlined, for example, red on pink, violet on lavender, or dark green on chartreuse. A certain amount of daring is required for this procedure, but the results are worth it. Always do a test piece first.

Outlining adds a personal touch to a banner. Like the amen to a prayer, the alleluia at Easter, or the artist's signature on a painting, it signifies completion.

DISPLAY

Improper display can diminish the finished project. Consequently, significant attention should be given to the way banners are hung.

Where practical, banners should be hung 3″–6″ away from the wall rather than flush against it. This lends depth and a feeling of life to the banner. Keep hanging methods as unobtrusive as possible, avoiding heavy cords, ropes, or chain.

Hung from the ceiling

Hang two lengths of clear fishing line from the sanctuary ceiling about 3′ apart and 6″ out from the wall. Tie S-hooks at each end where the top of the banner will be hung. (Be sure the points are level.) Drive small 4d box nails into the ends of a ¼″ dowel the width of the banner, leaving ½″ of the nails exposed. Slip the nails through the S-hooks to hang the banner. Changing banners is relatively easy, and the lines can be left in place when no banner is displayed because they are virtually invisible.

Attached to the wall

Valance curtain rods provide a practical alternative for both seasonal and permanent wall displays. Lengths can be adjusted to fit banners ranging in width from 26″–82″. They are supported by two small brackets and project 3″–5½″ from the wall. Adjustable spring-pressure curtain rods can be used the same way. They also come in variable lengths ranging from 36″–60″ to 48″–72″.

Freestanding

If wall space is limited, build a stand. However, be sure it has a rigid horizontal pole at the top to keep the banner from swinging or sliding (see illustration).

Procedure

1. All materials can be found at a building materials supplier. The vertical pole can be wood, metal, or PVC pipe. It should be at least a foot longer than any banner to be hung, as well as tall enough that a seated congregation can see the banner.

2. Look in plumbing supply stores for a PVC pipe T-fitting for the top of the pole. It should fit so tightly that gluing is unnecessary. Simple jam it onto one end of the pole and give it a few taps with a hammer.

3. For the crossbar, buy a wooden dowel the same diameter as the vertical pole, cut it in half, and jam the halves into the openings of the T-fitting.

4. For a base, cut ¼″ plywood into two squares—one 18″ × 18″ and one 12″ × 12″. Stack them and nail or screw them together. In the center, drill a hole the diameter of the vertical pole.

5. To hang the banner, cut a 1″ square notch

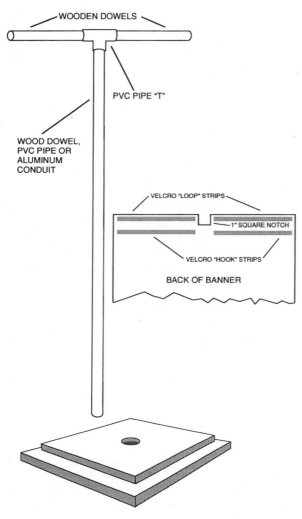

WOODEN DOWELS

PVC PIPE "T"

WOOD DOWEL,
PVC PIPE OR
ALUMINUM
CONDUIT

VELCRO "LOOP" STRIPS

1" SQUARE NOTCH

VELCRO "HOOK" STRIPS

BACK OF BANNER

in the center of the top edge of the banner.
Using Velcro adhesive, attach Velcro loop
strips to the top edge of the back of the banner
from the sides to the notch. Then attach
Velcro hook strips 3″ down from and parallel
to the top edge. (See the illustration above.)
Drape the banner over the top of the horizontal pole and mate the Velcro strips. This
method is practical, especially for processional
banners.

>>> Banners are works of art created to enhance
worship, encourage Christian action, and
glorify God. They should not be seen merely
as decorative adornments that add a note of
interest or a splash of color to otherwise drab
surroundings. Nor should they be seen as
elaborate craft projects.

>>> Bannermakers should be confident in their
work. There is no need for added gimmicks
such as fringe, tassels, or decorative ribbons,
which have a place on throw pillows,
draperies, and other home projects but are
unnecessary on banners. Not only do they
detract from the message of the designs, but
they also tend to become loose and unravel,
creating a maintenance problem.

USEFUL DESIGN TECHNIQUES

LETTERING PRINCIPLES

Letter spacing

Proper spacing of individual letters in a
word is vitally important to the overall appearance and readability of a banner. Inconsistent
or cramped spacing makes the viewer more
conscious of the letters than the words.

If every letter were rectangular, then spacing would be easy. It would be merely a matter
of measuring equal distances between rectangles, as with this group.

HMN

But the variety in widths and shapes of
individual letters makes simple measuring
impossible. The only pure rectangles in the
alphabet are *H*, *M*, and *N*. Look what happens
to the spacing when curved or irregular forms
are introduced:

NHAOCYTI

Everything seems out of place, especially
the *A* and *Y*. As these examples demonstrate,
letter spacing cannot be left to chance. Nor can
it be determined by a rigid set of rules. It is
done aesthetically, by eye, so the spaces appear

to be even. This is not as difficult as it sounds. The human eye is easily deceived.

Compare these two rectangles. Which is larger?

To most people, the vertical one appears to be larger, but actually both rectangles are the same size.

To space lettering correctly, imagine the blank areas between letters are filled with water and try to equalize the area the eye must "swim" to read from letter to letter. When lettering is properly spaced, the amount of liquid between letters appears to be the same.

Spaced by eye, the previous lettering appears as follows:

NHAOCYTI

The letters that need the most space between them are those made with single strokes such as *I* and *l*. They need breathing room to keep from appearing squashed.

illi

Slightly less space is needed between rectangular letters, for instance, *M* and *N*.

MN

A medium space is needed between a rectangular letter and a rounded letter, for example, *N* and *O* or *n* and *d*.

NO nd

Even less space is needed between two rounded letters, such as *O* and *C* or *b* and *o*.

OC bo

The odd but frequent combinations of *A* and *T, V* and *Y,* or *L* and *T* can virtually abut or even touch or overlap. Their distinctive shapes make them easy to distinguish.

AT VY LT

With letter spacing, there is actually only one absolute—set rules aside and trust the eye. Beginners usually space the letters too far apart, but the spacing becomes tighter with practice.

Letter size

The word *Christ* below illustrates another important lettering principle.

Christ

Christ

When guidelines are added, as in the second example, it becomes apparent that the letter forms with curves are relatively larger. This is standard practice for all lettering, both typeset and hand drawn. It is another necessary deception to compensate for the perception of the human eye.

For example, compare these two shapes without measuring. Which is taller?

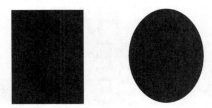

The rectangle appears taller to the eye, but measurement reveals that they are both the same height. Because of how the eye perceives rounded shapes, letters such as *C, G, J,* and *O* are always made slightly larger. On a banner this can be ¼″–1″ or even more, depending on the banner scale. Applying this principle will make the shapes appear more equal.

Word spacing

Use the width of an *N* as a starting point to determine the spacing of words, remembering that words, like letters, are spaced by eye and not by some arbitrary, regular measurement. It is possible to use narrower spacing if the work area is limited, but the words should never be so tightly spaced that they blend into alphabet soup nor so widely spaced that they lose their flow and readability. The only way to acquire this skill is to practice.

Line spacing

In general, the minimum amount of space between lines of lettering is the amount needed so the descenders of the letters in the upper line will not become confused with the ascenders of the letters in the lower line.

All things proclaim the existence of God

Notice how the *g* in the top line interferes with the *t* in the bottom line. It also is difficult to read. Below, the same lines are shown properly spaced.

All things proclaim the existence of God

Capital letters, which have no ascenders or descenders, can be spaced quite closely and still be distinguished.

HE HAS MADE ALL THINGS NEW

A short glossary of lettering terms

- *Ascenders*—The parts of lowercase letters extending above the main body, as on the letters *b*, *d*, *h*, *k*, for example.
- *Baseline*—The invisible guideline on which a line of lettering sits.
- *Descenders*—The parts of lowercase letters extending below the main body, as on the letters *g*, *j*, *p*, *q*, *y*, for example.
- *Lowercase*—Commonly know as small letters; so called because, in printing, these characters are kept in the lower cases or trays of type cabinets.
- *Sans serif*—A type style without serifs, for example,

Aa Bb Cc Dd Ee Ff Gg Hh Ii

- *Serif*—The decoration on the end of a letter stroke, for example,

Aa Bb Cc Dd Ee Ff Gg Hh Ii

- *Uppercase*—Commonly known as capital letters; so called because, in printing, these characters are kept in the upper cases or trays of type cabinets.

Lettering is an intricate and fascinating art. Keeping the principles of this section in mind makes it less difficult at first and easy later on.

LETTERING PATTERNS

Custom banners are often commissioned for weddings, anniversaries, or other special occasions where planning and construction time is limited. Often much of that valuable time is spent on patterns for the lettering. It would be easy to paint the words directly on the background, but paint and cloth are not that compatible and it is difficult to achieve a professional look this way. There are other lettering techniques, however, that do yield professional results with minimal effort.

Hand lettering

Materials

- Sheets of newsprint
- Masking tape or glue stick
- 12 oz. can of spray paint (red is a good contrast to the black print on the paper) *or* a pint of quick-drying enamel and an inexpensive 1"–1½" wide natural-bristle brush

Procedure

1. Glue or tape newspaper sheets together into one piece equal in size to the finished banner.
2. In a well-ventilated area (perhaps a garage), tack the paper sheet to the wall at eye level (or lay it on the floor). Keep extra sheets handy in case of mistakes.
3. a. *With spray paint:* Hold can 3″–6″ from the paper and write the words in order, starting at the upper left. A cursive style with simplified strokes generally works best. After drying, the strokes can be refined with a felt-tip marker.
3. b. *With enamel and brush:* Use the best possible block lettering style. Remember that mistakes are corrected easily during cutting.
4. Cut out letters and use like any other pattern.

The results of hand lettering are spontaneous and personal.

Book lettering

Materials

- A photocopier
- An X-Acto knife or a pair of sharp scissors
- A book on calligraphy, typography, or lettering that shows complete alphabets in different styles (section 745.6 of the local library should have a choice of such books)

Procedure

1. Photocopy the desired styles of lettering and add them to your design notebook. Be sure to include both uppercase and lowercase letters for each chosen alphabet. Bold styles work best. Look for sans serif typefaces such as Futura Display, Avant Garde, or Franklin Gothic. Look for serif typefaces such as Goudy Bold or Garamond Bold. As an alternative, look for simulated handwriting such as Kaufmann Script.
2. When lettering is needed for a project, for example, adding the names of the bride and groom to a wedding banner, choose an appropriate style from among the alphabets already stored in your design notebook.

3. Set the photocopier to its maximum enlargement percentage and copy the sample alphabet. Copy the enlargements successively until the letters are scaled to the required size. It will take several steps, but it is quicker and more accurate than tracing by hand.
4. Carefully cut out the individual letters with an X-Acto knife or sharp scissors.

The results of book lettering will be stylish and consistent.

Computer-generated lettering

This technique saves a lot of tracing and increases accessibility to a variety of lettering styles.

Materials

- A computer with a software package of various fonts
- A printer
- A photocopier

Procedure

1. Select the font and size of typeface (probably as large as possible, depending on the machine).
2. Type the words required for the banner and print them out. Save toner or ink by designating the font as an outline.
3. If necessary, enlarge the letters using a photocopier. Very large sizes may reproduce only one letter per sheet of paper.

Three lettering styles (complete alphabets or fonts, as today's computer-literate world would call them) are included on pages 20–22. They are especially helpful for creating custom banner designs and for personalizing a banner design by adding one or more names (for weddings, confirmations, graduations, etc.)

To use a selected style, enlarge the entire page on a photocopier set to its maximum enlargement percentage (156 percent for many copiers). If all the letters don't fit on a single page, copy them in sections. Copy each successive enlargement until the letters are the size required for the complete design.

AD LIB

ABCDEFG
HIJKLMN
OPQRSTU
VWXYZ
abcdefghi
jklmnopqr
stuvwxyz
& ?-,.

FRIZ QUADRATA

A B C D E F G H I J K
L M N O P Q R S T U
V W X Y Z & ? . , -
a b c d e f g h i j k l m
n o p q r s t u v w x y z

A B C D E F G H I J K
L M N O P Q R S T U
V W X Y Z & ? . , -
a b c d e f g h i j k l m
n o p q r s t u v w x y z

FUTURA

A B C D E F G H I J K
L M N O P Q R S T U
V W X Y Z & ? . , '
a b c d e f g h i j k l m
n o p q r s t u v w x y z

A B C D E F G H I J
K L M N O P Q R S T
U V W X Y Z & ? . , '
a b c d e f g h i j k l m
n o p q r s t u v w x y z

COLOR PRINCIPLES

Coordinating colors

There are several ways to coordinate colors for a banner.

A color wheel can be useful, but it also carries the danger of turning what could be an artistic process into merely a mechanical one.

Another place to turn for ready-to-go color combinations is a fabric dealer. Pay particular attention to floral prints and other multicolored fabrics. Purchase narrow strips of the best of them and add them to your design notebook. Borrow three or four colors from one of the swatches when other ideas do not seem to work.

The best place to look is the natural world, where the glories of God's creation appear in infinitely beautiful combinations. Sunrises reveal magentas, purples, peaches, reds, oranges, pinks, blues, and yellows. They give way to a sky filled with shades of blue, gray, and white. From there turn to the purple and blue mountains, green trees with brown trunks, and flowers combining variegated greens with reds, yellows, oranges, violets, and pinks. Nature provides a color wheel to stir the imagination. Use a camera to capture especially striking color combinations and add them to your design notebook.

Seasonal color

Early in the Bible, color was connected with meaningful worship. Beginning in Exodus 26:1, God, through Moses, instructs the Israelites to "make the tabernacle with ten curtains of finely twisted linen and blue, purple and scarlet yarn."

The early church apparently used white throughout the year. Color to differentiate the seasons appeared gradually between the ninth and 13th centuries. It was not until the 16th century, however, that the church established the now familiar sequence of red, green, violet, black, and white. Because of their inherent moods and characteristics, these colors have subtly influenced worship for many decades.

Red (5) is the warm color of life-giving blood. It is passion, love, caring, and sentimentality, but it also can be anger, subjugation, and war. Of all the colors of worship, it is the most powerful. A large splash of red demands attention. In liturgy, the church reserves red to commemorate Pentecost, Reformation, Palm Sunday, ordinations, and the days of various saints. These festivals, representing high emotion and God's call to action, like the color, cannot be ignored.

Green (14), the church's nonfestival color, designates the two transitional periods known as "after the Epiphany" and "after Pentecost." This implies these periods are routine and unexciting. It is better to think of them as times of learning and growth in faith, times that challenge artists to find different and exciting ways to lend visual emphasis to the rich variety of messages from Jesus' ministry. Here, the vibrancy of the greens chosen is essential. These seasons call for the deep natural shades of summer leaves and grass.

The Western world associates **black (2)** with mourning, absence, darkness, and death. The church uses it only for Good Friday. For bannermakers, however, it is an excellent background color. Virtually all other colors seem to advance, to pop out, when placed against it. Use black with restraint because its effect can be overwhelming.

White (1) is the festival color of the church. It is reserved for celebrations that reflect themes of purity, light, innocence, holiness, and redemption, including Jesus' birth, baptism, transfiguration, and resurrection, as well as Maundy Thursday and Thanksgiving. For the bannermaker it presents challenges. Although it is easy to use for letters and other design elements, as a background, white can be intimidating. It tends to dominate, forcing boldness in the choice of colors and graphics. Timidity in the presence of white only results in design elements that get lost.

Violet (20) most often is associated with the Lenten season. As a combination of warm red (passion) and cool blue (calm), neither moving nor still, violet perfectly represents this season that refocuses us from Jesus' hopeful birth to His agonizing death. Violet is preferable to purple for Lent because purple suggests the pagan Roman imperium. Violet gives a truer portrayal of Lent's themes of humility, penitence, sorrow, and grief.

Blue (19) best represents the other season of thoughtful preparation, Advent. It gives Advent its own identity. In a worship setting, blue creates an atmosphere akin to that of darkness becoming light, of a new day dawning filled with possibilities. Like black, it is very accommodating and works well with virtually any color. There is no better color to signify the beginning of the church year.

The nonliturgical color **yellow (11)** endows the worship environment with the glow and warmth of the sun. Used for Easter, it generates thoughts of the enlightening revelation of Jesus' empty tomb that vanquishes death and despair forever.

Throughout the church year, the varying colors used in worship unfold like a rainbow, affirming the constant presence of God's grace in the life of the individual Christian. Like Joseph's many-colored coat, the colors signify the believer as God's firstborn and heir to His promise of eternal life.

DESIGN PRINCIPLES

Brainstorming method

The best way to get creative juices flowing and thus come up with a great idea for a banner design is to use the process of brainstorming, otherwise known as thumbnailing. With notebook or sketch pad in hand, quickly sketch lots of ideas as fast as possible, no matter how radical or improbable. Remember, nothing is more limiting than one idea. Thumbnails, as the term implies, should be small (about 2″) so they all fit on one or two pages. When there are at least 10 ideas, sift them and begin eliminating ideas until only two or three are left. Enlarge and polish these, refining graphic forms and lines and sorting through possible colors. Next, pick the best one of these, turn it into a line drawing (like the ones in this book), and copy it onto an overhead projector transparency. It is now possible to transform that idea into a physical reality.

A key component of the creative process is flexibility. The mind needs to be kept open to possibilities. As work proceeds, continue to question, explore, and adapt. Would an element work better in a different color? Would a rough or smooth texture accent a particular area? Does the addition of this shape upset the overall design? Is the slogan too long? These are just a few of the questions that might be asked and, if the answer to any is yes, acted upon.

Creating a social ministry banner

Are you involved in a volunteer service organization or social ministry that needs an increased public awareness? A banner might bring your special cause to the forefront or, at the very least, generate discussion.

Materials

- Background cloth (felt is a good choice because it does not require lining) in either dark blue, burgundy, or dark green (these colors provide a good contrast to most other colors)
- Iron-on adhesive, sufficient to cover the background
- ½ yard each of three or four different colors of a mostly cotton fabric (such as broadcloth) for the lettering and design pieces (as an alternative, pick through the fabric scraps you have collected to find colors that stand out against the background)
- Sharp scissors
- Iron, pressing cloth, and assorted items needed for finishing (pins, sewing machine, etc.)

Procedure

1. Pick a size for the banner—2′ × 8′ or 3′ × 6′ are good proportions.
2. Cut the background to size, adding necessary allowances for the hem and casing. Place *face side up* on the work surface.
3. Pick a word theme. If your ministry uses a slogan, start there. A hymnal is an excellent source for concise, meaningful phrases. Several stanzas from hymns immediately come to mind: "Give me the courage to speak when strong oppress the weak"; "The victims of injustice cry for shelter and food"; "Forbid that we not care." Also scan the collects and prayers of the day in the front of hymnals for ideas such as "For those held unjustly bring release." As an alternative,

open the Bible to the Psalms, Song of Songs, Ecclesiastes, or one of the prophetic books (Isaiah or Jeremiah). Begin reading through the verses and, without analyzing them, jot down any phrases that strike a responsive chord. Do not stop with one.

4. Begin sifting through the choices, tossing out the inappropriate ones or rewriting them until there is one phrase that suits the banner. With a large marker, write it down as a reminder while work proceeds.

5. For the lettering, use patterns saved from other projects and randomly select the necessary letters. (It doesn't matter if they are not the same style.) Arrange them on the background to see how they work together. As an alternative, experiment with one of the quick-lettering techniques described or use one of the furnished alphabet styles. ("Ad Lib" is a good choice.)

6. Place the iron-on adhesive *paper side up* on a flat surface. Reverse the letter patterns and trace them with a pencil. Space them closely to minimize waste.

7. Cut out the letters and fuse them to the back of the fabric scraps. (Consider using a mixture of colors.) After they cool, cut around the fused letters and peel off the paper backing. Arrange the letters on the background material in a tightly spaced block roughly covering the center of the banner.

8. On the remainder of the adhesive sheet, sketch a variety of silhouette shapes. They can be geometric (squares, circles, triangles), linear (curves, zig-zags, straight orthogonals), or natural (flowers, leaves, or other plant forms). Let the chosen phrase suggest ideas or look at the designs in this book for inspiration. Bond the shapes to the fabric pieces and let them cool. Peel off the paper backing and arrange the designs on the banner with the letters. Often just the process of doing a preliminary arrangement will suggest possibilities for other shapes.

9. As you move the design elements around looking for a pleasing arrangement, keep in mind that spaces are either positive or negative. Positive space is the shape itself. Negative space is the empty area around the shape and is as important to a successful design as the positive space. Not all the negative space needs to be filled. Watch the negative spaces change as the shapes are moved to new positions. Instead of lumping the lines of letters into a single block, split them and work the shapes between the lines of lettering. Or turn the lettering block at an angle. This is the time to experiment and learn because nothing is fastened permanently. It often helps to stand up, walk around, and look at your work from a different perspective—even upside down.

10. Finalize the arrangement. Be sure the letters are properly spaced and that none of the shapes is accidentally placed *adhesive side up*. Preheat the iron. Follow the instructions for bonding that come with the iron-on adhesive. To ready the banner for display, add hems to the top and bottom.

FINDING A NICHE

No matter how a banner is conceived and executed, it is important to keep its ultimate purpose in mind. Banners are designed to play an important part in worship or social ministry, and they do that best when they are well placed.

Frequently, banners are displayed only in the vicinity of the altar. But not all worship-related activities take place directly in the front. When worshipers turn to observe the choir, are their eyes confronted by an expanse of blank wall? As guests and members leave a meaningful worship experience, does the narthex or hallway outside the sanctuary serve only as egress to the parking lot? These are only two areas that bannermakers can use subtly to extend the worship experience, to enhance awareness of social ministry, or to invite participation in other church activities.

Remember, banners are meant to excite, provoke thought, and create an atmosphere conducive to worship and social action. Part of what makes banners interesting is that once they are displayed, people not only see them, they experience them, and depending on their personal outlook, draw different messages from them.

Beyond These Walls

The Spirit of the Sovereign LORD is on me, because the LORD has anointed me to preach good news to the poor. He has sent me to bind up the brokenhearted, to proclaim freedom for the captives and release from darkness for the prisoners. (Isaiah 61:1)

Going back at least to the time of Isaiah, God's chosen people have been given the responsibility to bring healing and reconciliation to a troubled world. As we share God's Word and announce the forgiveness we have through Jesus, our Savior, we spread the message of our heavenly Father's actions on our behalf. We reach out in love *beyond the walls* of our houses and churches because God has demonstrated His saving love for us in Christ.

This initial design lends visual reality to our commission to spread the Good News through word and deed.

BACKGROUND (4)

Awaken our hearts to your love for the poor and needy

LETTERING (8)

1

1

1

1

1

1

1

1

20

24

5

5

5

24

20

Awaken Our Hearts to Your Love for the Poor and Needy

In this visual prayer, we ask God to change our perspective from a self-serving outlook to one directed toward serving others.

Because the white (1) hearts overlap one another, they need to be outlined. Use one of the techniques listed on page 14 under the heading "Outlining design elements." To add depth to the design, use a red washable marking pen to shade the white (1) hearts (see the shaded areas in the design). Using an inexpensive water-color paintbrush, dampen the marking pen lines with tap water. The marker will bleed and create a subtle shading.

An Open Hand in Times of Need Is the Rarest of Gifts

To approach someone with an open hand indicates trustworthiness, a desire to take the first step, a willingness to share. It also says the approach is unconditional with no desire to take anything in return. An outstretched hand invites those in need to reach out and take the offered help. By making the initial move, we dissipate fear and open doors.

As sinners, we were in desperate need, lost and alone. But God sent His Son, Jesus, to earth in human form. He knew our sorrows and joys. When Jesus died, He stretched out His hands for us. Nails pierced them. Now He stretches out His risen hand to guide us safely through this world to the mansion He has prepared for us in heaven. We can offer nothing in payment. It is God's gift to us through the nail-pierced hands of His Son. Now God asks us to share this gift and all that we have with others. On that last day, may He praise us for unknowingly feeding, clothing, or visiting our Savior.

This design imposes no special conditions on the viewer. Its simplicity demands nothing more than acceptance.

ALL NUMBERS (9)

LETTERING (12)

BACKGROUND (23)

Time: A Gift to Spend in Service to Others

Galatians 4:4 states that "when the time had fully come," God sent Jesus to earth to live, work, teach, preach, and finally to die and rise again. He chose to give us the greatest gift—His Son—to complete His plan of salvation. Now, we have the opportunity to use the time God gives us on earth to honor and glorify Him.

After many years outside the work force, a friend felt the need to get back into the "real" world, so she got a job. Now she has quit her full-time position. She said she doesn't need piles of money. She has discovered more fulfillment in devoting time to causes important to her than in bringing home a big paycheck. To what causes do you give your precious time? How do these choices honor God and reflect His love to those around you?

Statistics prove that those who give of their time live longer, happier lives. Perhaps more important than a longer life, devoting time in service to others allows you freedom of expression. In what creative ways do you use your time? How might you spend time in creative pursuits for God?

After viewing this design, a friend asked why I didn't place the numbers as they appear on a clock face. I answered that the numbers represent not only minutes and hours, but days, weeks, months, and years. Service to others is not measured in units of time but in actions. Ask God to bless your use of time.

Good Works Blossom into Miracles of Grace

While searching for phrases to use on these banners, the lack of stories about people who perform acts of kindness amazed me. Maybe those who do good heed Jesus' words in Matthew 6:2 and do not "announce it with trumpets." Or maybe violent acts draw a larger audience.

It would be nice, though, if someone would blow the trumpet for those who make kind deeds a natural part of life. Acts of kindness may not increase revenue or viewer ratings, but humanity needs to see the positive effects of love. More important than the actions or the awareness of the actions, we need to share the *motivation* for our good works. We act not to gain favor with God or with people, but to celebrate the faith God has worked in our hearts. Through our rebirth in Christ, God has created us for good works. He sends His Holy Spirit to accomplish this purpose in us.

Outline all flower parts (labeled 7, 8, 11, and 12) with a permanent red marker. Outline all leaves and stems with a permanent dark green marker. To add depth to the design, use washable marking pens to shade the parts of the flowers following the method described on page 15. Use red to shade the flower petals, orange to shade the parts of the flower centers, and dark green to shade the leaves and stems (see the shaded areas in the design).

BACKGROUND (11)

Good works blossom into miracles of grace

LETTERING (4)

ALL PLANT
LEAVES
& STEMS
(14)

11 12

7

12
12 12
12
12
11
8 12
12 12
7

LETTERING (12)

BACKGROUND (21 OR 22)

FLOWER
STEMS (14)

A Time to Mourn

There is a time for everything, and a season for every activity under heaven: ... a time to weep and a time to laugh, a time to mourn and a time to dance. (Ecclesiastes 3:1, 4)

These next two designs provide a visual statement about loss. As the Bible says, there is a time to mourn. It is a natural part of the grief process. But just as the dead of winter gives way to the new life of spring, so our tears can and will give way to laughter, dancing, and joy. As Christians, we have the sure hope of new life because of Christ's death and resurrection. Nothing can separate us from the God who made this promise and will keep it.

To add depth to the flowers, use washable marking pens to shade the flower petals and stems (see the shaded areas in the design). Using an inexpensive watercolor paintbrush, dampen the marking pen lines with tap water. The marker will bleed and create a subtle shading.

You Turn My Mourning into Dancing and Fill My Heart with Joy

Thou hast turned ... my mourning into dancing; Thou hast loosed my sackcloth and girded me with gladness. (Psalm 30:11 RSV)

I based this design on a banner originally developed for Christmas. Why speak of mourning during a time of joy? I needed to express my emotional response to the significant losses our faith community had experienced during the previous year: our congregation's vice president had died tragically; two new members had lost their husbands to cancer; and a car/train accident had taken the lives of several teenagers. Other members had faced death, a broken marriage, or job loss. Greeting cards seemed too impersonal to express my grief.

When I've experienced significant loss, the best gift I have received was a hug. This banner is a visual "hug" for those who grieve. It speaks words of hope. Joy will return after the grief is processed. The message of Christmas is the same message as Easter: Our earthly life will include problems and death, but through God's grace, we have the gift of salvation and the promise of eternal life. Our temporal sadness will turn to everlasting joy.

To add depth to the flowers, use washable marking pens to shade the flower petals and stems following the method described on page 15 (see the shaded areas in the design).

BACKGROUND (5)

IN MY GRIEF BE MY STRENGTH

LETTERING (12)

In My Grief Be My Strength

Grief is forced on us by significant loss, such as unemployment, death, or divorce. The burdens imposed by grief can seem unbearable. Grief leaves us feeling vulnerable. It shatters our sense of stability.

When we grieve, we often find ourselves making strident pleas for God's immediate action. But grief is a process with stages that have no time limits. But those who are grieving do not have to "go it alone." To support those who are grieving, we can honor the loss, respect the grief, listen.

Periods of mourning offer us an opportunity to share the message that Jesus has walked this path. Before Jesus called Lazarus from the grave, He wept. Jesus allowed Himself to mourn, even though He could have called Lazarus back to life at any moment. Jesus understands the process of grief and will guide our words and actions to reflect His love and care. This banner is a visual prayer, a reminder to turn to God for strength in times of grief.

This design can be combined with the next four designs to form a litany of hope for those grieving over a death, the breakup of a marriage, the loss of a job, a life-changing diagnosis, or for those dealing with the results of violence. These banners are also a call to action.

Plead for the Widow

Learn to do good; seek justice, correct oppression; defend the fatherless, plead for the widow. (Isaiah 1:17 RSV)

Anyone who thinks the Old Testament has no relevance to contemporary issues needs to read Isaiah. This was among the first books I read when I needed inspiration for these designs. There are enough themes in just the above verse to inspire a series of banners. If you need a theme banner that speaks about conflict resolution, try "Come now, let us reason together" (Isaiah 1:18). Read further in Isaiah and you will find many verses appropriate for social ministry banners.

In biblical times, the loss of a husband placed a woman at the mercy of a society that valued her solely as a wife, child producer, and caretaker. Isaiah 1:17 is one of several Bible passages that express concern for the plight of widows. Consider, for example, "Cursed is the man who withholds justice from the alien, the fatherless or the widow" (Deuteronomy 27:19). Even Jesus spoke to the plight of widows as with His dying breaths He entrusted Mary to John. In so doing, Jesus spoke volumes about our responsibility to those who face the prospect of life alone. While Isaiah 1:17 specifically refers to widows, the theme can be applied to anyone grieving the loss of a loved one.

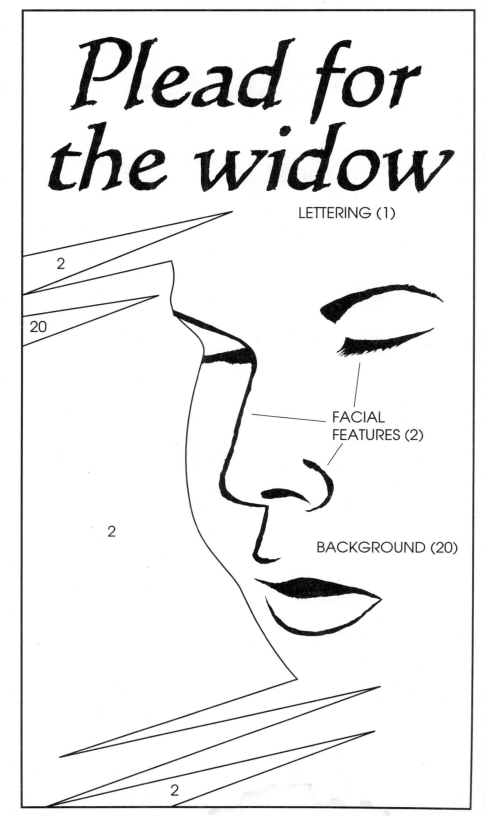

LETTERING AND FACE (2)

BACKGROUND (11)

Strengthen the Weak

I will search for the lost and bring back the strays. I will bind up the injured and strengthen the weak. (Ezekiel 34:16)

The Psalms and the Old Testament prophetic books are among the best sources for meaningful, appropriate verses for banner designs that pertain to social ministry concerns.

This design is a simple, visual reminder that God is present in our lives. In fact, God sent Jesus to walk among us. His victory over sin, death, and the grave assures us that nothing this world can throw at us can overcome those whom God calls His own. Through the apostle Paul, God reminds us that in our weakness, His power is made perfect.

God's Strength Is Perfected in Weakness

While finalizing the color choices for this design, I began to reflect on my life. As I relived certain events, tears slowly formed. I told myself I couldn't let this happen, but my vision blurred, making it difficult to see the images on my computer monitor. I realized that I needed to deal with those feelings in some positive way.

First, I wrote a letter expressing my disappointment over a bitter situation. Then I called an old friend about something that I perceived had caused a rift between us. To date, I haven't received a reply to the letter (I don't anticipate one), but the relationship with my friend has been reconciled.

We often view tears as a sign of weakness, but tears serve a purpose. They show that we have tried but failed. Then, in the midst of our weakness, God works His miracle. He takes away our weaknesses and replaces them with the strength of Christ. With the Holy Spirit's guidance, we are able to move forward.

Outline the stem pieces with a dark green marker. Follow the procedure on page 14. A ¼" wide line works best. Outline each flower petal with a red washable marking pen, following the method described on page 15.

LETTERING (1)

Calm the Fearful

Inspiration for this design came from two passages:

[Jesus] replied, "You of little faith, why are you so afraid?" Then He got up and rebuked the winds and the waves, and it was completely calm. (Matthew 8:26)

Say to those with fearful hearts, "Be strong, do not fear." (Isaiah 35:4)

Those who have no faith are like the disciples, tossed by the winds and waves of indecision or fear. They see no solution. What wonderful news we have to share! We have the solution to the fear of entering a strange environment or starting a new job. We know that Jesus has calmed the storms, both natural and spiritual. Through His presence in our lives, we can stand firm and be strong. In the brilliance of Easter morning, He conquered sin, death, and the grave for us. What do we have to fear if our all-powerful God is on our side?

When others are in pain, often the simple knowledge of your presence is all that's needed. Nonjudgmental words, a listening ear, a ready hand, and a healing touch in the form of a gentle hug are highly valued. Gradually, trust develops and you can ease into a troubled life and share the answer to the cry for help— Jesus.

Though I Walk through the Valley of the Shadow of Death

We know that life has its ups and downs, but we fervently pray that our life will have few if any low points. But God has never promised us an "easy" life. Because we are His children, we are not automatically protected from illness, heartache, job loss, or death. Christians can and do suffer.

But we don't need to fear anything the devil or this world might throw at us. God has promised to walk with us through everything—even the valley of the shadow of death. Notice the last phrase "the *shadow* of death." Yes, this human body will die, but it is a passage—a shadow. Christ's death and resurrection assures believers that those who fall asleep in Christ will rise to new life. Therefore, we ask the Holy Spirit to strengthen our faith and bring us safely through the valleys to the bright mountaintop of God's glorious New Jerusalem.

This banner is both a reminder to Christians of God's promise and a call to share this promise. As we receive chemotherapy, visit a nursing home, or work in an AIDS hospice, we can demonstrate God's love and continual presence. We can be His hands to comfort, His feet to run errands, His ears to listen, and His eyes to cry. The Holy Spirit will bless our witness.

Lift the Clouds of Fear and Hate

The world seems lost in a fog of hate and fear. We watch aggression and paranoia take over other countries and worry that the same may happen here.

When the Christian church started, factions took sides about the inclusion of Gentiles and Samaritans in the body of Christ. But Paul preached that in this church "Christ is all, and is in all" (Colossians 3:11). We need to ask God to remind us daily that we are all members of His creation.

This design illustrates creative use of randomly selected letter forms. If you can't come up with the perfect graphic element to express an idea, then consider a "words only" format. Try a "ransom note" approach. Randomly choose the letters from patterns saved from other projects. Mix fonts and sizes to create a feeling of spontaneous joy.

This design and the next four designs focus on differences. While these banners address issues of intolerance, racism, or hatred, they also call us to celebrate our unity in Christ, the uniqueness of God's creation, and the gifts He gives each of us through His Spirit. Consider different ways to pair these designs to present visual statements about God's love for all people and our personal response to His saving love.

Let Us Also Walk in the Spirit

The fruit of the Spirit is love, joy, peace, patience, kindness, goodness, faithfulness, gentleness and self-control. (Galatians 5:22–23)

Racism is an ugly word. Unfortunately, it seems to be a constant in human interaction. The media constantly report attacks on "outsiders." Some people appear to be guided by hatred of others based solely on skin color or beliefs.

Even the people of Jesus' day experienced racism. Jews would not associate with their cousins, the Samaritans. Yet Jesus explained that when God's love dwells in us, we want to share it with everyone, no matter their skin color, style of dress, or accent.

Perhaps the worst part of racism is that no one is born a racist or bigot. Racism is passed down from generation to generation. Our children learn by our example. Before we chastise others for their prejudices, what prejudices do we need to ask God to help us overcome?

When God's Spirit lives in us, He enables us to turn away from our prejudices, leave behind our hatred of others. Instead, the Holy Spirit works in us to bear fruit that is pleasing to our heavenly Father. When we rely on God to guide our actions, we respond to others in love and joy, work for peace, act kindly and gently, and exhibit patience and self-control.

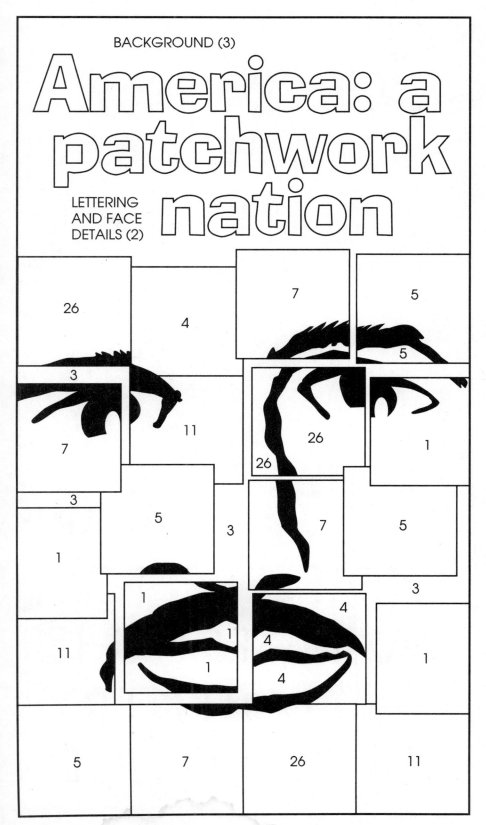

BACKGROUND (3)

America: a patchwork nation

LETTERING
AND FACE
DETAILS (2)

America: A Patchwork Nation

Boatloads of Cuban and Haitian refugees dot the Caribbean, fleeing oppression and poverty. Mexicans sneak across the border to a land of plenty. Would-be Americans stand in lines at embassies, hoping for a new start. For many, the United States is the land of opportunity. One immigrant from Africa said he left his homeland to live in a state of peace. Another recent immigrant said America offers unique opportunities not available in other countries.

America is a land of immigrants—a patchwork nation. Most of us ignore the fact that everyone who lives here came from somewhere else. Even Native Americans probably descended from immigrants who crossed from Siberia to Alaska on a land bridge that now lies beneath the Bering Sea. The millions of people who came here have made their adopted country stronger and more diverse.

How do we treat those who arrive on these shores looking for a new life and willing to contribute to our community? How can the church play a more active role in welcoming, settling, and integrating immigrants? How does God call us to share His love through word and action with these newcomers?

Our Differences Manifest the Artistry of God

At one time, American culture was considered a great "melting pot" in which other cultures were stirred and absorbed. These days, American culture is often spelled with a hyphen. On MTV a popular Cuban-American singer performs her latest song. A local theater premiers a film based on a novel by a Chinese-American, while across town a modern dance company displays the latest vision of a Jamaican-American choreographer. And an opening at the art museum displays the latest paintings by Asian-American artists who emigrated from Vietnam, Thailand, and Korea.

And that's just the beginning. Contemporary America seems more like a giant cultural street fair—a variety of clothing, food, and people displayed on common sidewalks. Just as the early church welcomed and benefited from the many ethnic groups that God brought to faith, our country benefits from the fresh ideas and new outlooks hyphenated Americans bring. After all, God has created each person with unique gifts and talents and each has his or her place in this world and, for believers, in the body of Christ. So let's celebrate and enjoy God's great masterpiece!

LETTERING (19)

BACKGROUND (4)

OUR DIFFERENCES MANIFEST THE ARTISTRY OF GOD

CROSS (11)

ALL LETTERING (1)

Isn't There eNough hATE in the world?

BACKGROUND (3)

Isn't There Enough Hate in the World?

Turn the pages of any newspaper, or flip the channel on the remote, and you'll find stories of violent actions committed by individuals or groups against other individuals or groups. Every day extremists hide behind the First Amendment as they vent their hatred on public-access channels. A recent report stated that hate crimes in one southern city have more than doubled over the previous four years.

Hatred breeds hatred. Long-standing prejudices eventually escalate into war or other acts of violence. Just look at recent history in Northern Ireland, Bosnia, or Oklahoma City. The nightmare of what could happen if extremist groups prevail compels us to speak against hatred and share God's message of love and reconciliation in Jesus Christ.

This design is done in the style of painted graffiti to better express the meaning of the words. While graffiti has been used for centuries, sometimes as a positive art form or historical record, modern graffiti is often senseless vandalism. Consider spray-painted gang signs that mark territories or hastily painted swastikas on synagogue doors. Here, however, a cross covers the graffiti, pointing us to our Savior. In Him, our heavenly Father counters the hate of this world with His all-powerful love.

Help Us See Others through Your Eyes

Racial prejudice surrounds us. We think we're above it all, but sometimes it sneaks into our language or attitudes.

Lest we think the United States is innocent of such prejudice, consider World War II. United States officials forced Japanese-Americans to liquidate their assets and relocate to detention camps. The same rule was not applied to those with German or Italian ancestry. And even as we think the Civil Rights Movement has made great strides toward racial equality, one high-ranking New York official said, "It makes me sizzle, because ... no matter what I accomplish as an individual, I will always be judged by what people see first, my color." He had just been mistaken for a mugger because he happened to be black.

God does not look at our outward appearance. He looks at our hearts. And because we stand in the light of Jesus' cross, we are all the same to God—His dearly loved children. This design is a visual prayer that God would move us to a life of tolerance and mutual respect. This banner is an appeal for God's help to bring about the day when all people will live together in peace and harmony. It is a plea for God to keep us from judging one another based on skin color.

UPPER
LETTERING (1)

LETTERING
BLOCK (2)

Peace on Earth—Let It Begin with Me

We pray repeatedly for a cessation of hostilities in strife-torn areas of the world such as former communist nations, Northern Ireland, and the Middle East. Locally, we appeal to government officials for help to settle disputes in our neighborhoods, halt gang and domestic violence, or curb crime.

We often forget, though, that as Christians we have a gift for the world. In fact, we have been charged with the task of sharing this gift with those around us. The night before Jesus died, He told His disciples, "Peace I leave with you; My peace I give you" (John 14:27). Part of knowing Christ is knowing the peace only He can bring. When we share Christ with others, we become God's instruments to bring peace to a violent world. In the words of the song, "Let there be peace on earth, and let it begin with me."

Gone Fishing

In light of Jesus' invitation in Matthew 4:19 to "Come, follow Me, … and I will make you fishers of men," the phrase "Gone Fishing" struck me as the perfect expression of evangelism.

What would prompt me to include this design with others directly related to social ministry? The answer is simple. By His life and ministry, Jesus showed that actions speak louder than words. While bringing His message of God's grace and love, Jesus ministered to the physical needs of the crowds. He fed the hungry, healed lepers, and sent demons packing. As a result, "large crowds … followed Him" (Matthew 4:25). As He saw to physical needs, He also taught the crowds, sharing the message of salvation.

Jesus invites us to join Him on a great fishing trip, but He doesn't want us to forget the bags of canned goods, boxes of diapers, warm coats—anything that might remove the obstacles so the ears of our "crowd" can hear the message of God's saving grace.

Wisdom Is with the Aged

Wisdom is with the aged, and understanding in length of days. (Job 12:12 RSV)

Older friends such as Don, Jerry, Curt, and Irmgard (to name a few) constantly remind me of the wisdom and joy age brings. Don always greets me with a ready hug and a huge grin. Jerry shares his love of God's Word when he reads lessons during worship and relates pertinent background information gleaned from years of Bible study. Curt relates his latest travel adventures with great gusto while his wife, Irmgard, updates us on her grandchildren with the same obvious joy. And my parents are always there with support and a listening ear.

Autumn leaves are the perfect symbol for this design. Seen against the sun, a seemingly lifeless leaf reveals a special brilliance. Browns become bronzes highlighted by glowing shades of scarlet, orange, gold, and green. Each leaf is unique, a special reminder that older adults have gained wisdom from which we can learn a great deal if we listen.

BACKGROUND (2)

WISDOM IS WITH THE AGED

LETTERING (12)

Lives Turned Upside Down

Unemployment is all about the loss of comfort zones such as daily commutes, paychecks, work spaces, and co-workers who have become good friends. Because we often identify who we are with what we do, job loss, whether expected or unexpected, raises questions of self-worth and ability. We don't know what to do, who we are, or where to go when we've lost a job.

Like other significant losses, unemployment imposes a period of grief. But circumstances seldom allow time to process this grief. There are ads to search, résumés and cover letters to send, interviews to prepare for, and a host of other challenges. Job loss not only devastates the person, it upsets the lives of immediate family members. Tensions rise as income and savings dwindle.

As we pursue a new job, it may help to remember that without the accents, *résumé* becomes *resume*. Therefore, as you prepare your résumé, you also can resume living. You have a chance to resume what God always intended for you to do.

The lower portion of the banner is filled with symbols representing occupations. For example, "2+3=5" stands for teaching. The "RN" represents nursing. Feel free to substitute symbols more appropriate for your setting.

BACKGROUND (4)

BACKGROUND (22)

ALL LETTERING (1)

Admit you're powerless

God turns lives around

Admit You're Powerless—God Turns Lives Around

It's hard to speak about substance abuse because I've had little personal experience with it or its consequences. I did have a roommate in the service who, upon returning to the barracks each night, took a few quick belts from a bottle of vodka. Several drunken incidents brought reductions in rank and other punitive measures. When challenged to seek help, my roommate repeatedly stated he could quit anytime. We asked him to prove it, but during our time together, he never did. According to his statements, this man believed he had control of his situation. His actions showed otherwise.

It's difficult to admit you're powerless. We don't want to admit that something or someone else has control of our lives. For Christians, admitting powerlessness is actually a sign of strength. On our own, we can't fight against Satan's temptations. Instead, we are drawn further and further into his grasp. But God has taken control of our lives. He has sent His Holy Spirit to work faith in our hearts. Our strong God sent His only Son, Jesus, to defeat the devil and win the victory over sin and death. Because Jesus is in control of our lives, we have the power to defeat our addictions, but only when we rely on Him.

God, Show Me the Way I Should Go

We all face decisions. Which school to attend, whether to look for a new job, and questions about relationships are just a few examples of the issues that confront us. Some choices are clear. But sometimes it seems as though we're in a dark forest and we've lost the path. We don't know which choice to make, which direction to take.

It is precisely at these times that God reminds us that He's in control. He has a plan for our lives. When we ask for God's guidance, He will show us the way to go.

This particular design was inspired by a mountain hike I took. The trail passed a dense stand of aspens. The splashes of vibrant orange and yellow-gold leaves split by vertical lines of white tree trunks left an indelible image on my mind. As I walked across a carpet of undisturbed leaves, I felt as though I were walking through a giant stained-glass cathedral. As I walked that path, I realized I had no control over the scene. I was experiencing a gift from God—a path He had chosen for me.

SCRIPT
LETTERING
BLOCK (11)

BACKGROUND (2)

We Have Bread Enough to Spare, Yet Others Perish with Hunger

This design was inspired by several newspaper and magazine articles and Jesus' miraculous feeding of the 4,000 (Matthew 15:29–38, especially v. 32).

One article described the contrasts in one South American city. In a posh neighborhood, a delicatessen displays wheels of cheese the size of sofa cushions. In a poorer part of town, hundreds of people in tattered clothes rummage through the city's garbage dumps. Another article quoted a woman from a war-torn country in southern Europe. She said that there's no longer a future, only a struggle for immediate survival.

God knows our needs. Daily He provides all that we require for this life. When Jesus walked this earth, He healed people and even fed the crowds that followed Him. In His Supper, Jesus gives us of His own body and blood—a life-sustaining gift that strengthens us for the tasks ahead. It is Jesus' sacrifice that motivates us to share both our bread and the Good News of the Bread of Life.

To show the contrast between abundance and deprivation, this design uses two contrasting letter styles. One is bold with tight spacing. The other is a rough script style.

They Have No Certain Dwellingplace

Even unto this present hour we both hunger, and thirst, and are naked, and are buffeted, and have no certain dwelling-place. (1 Corinthians 4:11 KJV)

"It's bitterly cold," the television anchor states. "Our reporter is with the police as they search for the homeless, who have only a few blankets or maybe a dog to keep them warm. But the mayor's office tells us there aren't enough shelters. And some people don't want the help. They don't want to be told what to do."

We may not be able to force anyone to accept help, but we can provide shelter or food when asked for it. We can supply blankets, warm clothes, and food. For those whose dignity has been stripped away, we need to find ways to respect what self-esteem is left.

More important, how do we communicate to those without a permanent shelter that we *do* have a certain dwellingplace? We have God's promise of refuge, both in this world and in our spiritual life. We need to explore methods of sharing the Gospel with those who do not have a home, a car, or enough food. Yes, the Holy Spirit can work in a person's heart when he or she is cold or hungry, but the Holy Spirit also will work through us to answer these physical needs.

BACKGROUND (4)

The Victims Cry for Shelter and Food

Major disasters focus our attention. We rush to meet the immediate needs of victims by organizing fund drives and appealing for donations of food, clothing, and necessities. One magazine article stated that disasters really motivate people.

As we provide the necessities for earthly life, we also need to find ways to share the necessities for spiritual life. Consider including tracts or Bibles or other religious literature in care packages. Are there ways to partner with other churches or religious organizations to provide counseling during natural disasters or other calamities? Take every opportunity to pray for those affected by the disaster. Place them in God's hands for the healing of both body and spirit. Keep in mind that as we help those in need, we are helping Jesus (Matthew 25:31–46).

Specifically addressing disaster relief, this banner also might be applicable for a world mission program. This design is an open-ended challenge to the viewer. Others may take a different approach to depicting these words. I chose to let the message dominate and incorporate simple pictorial elements—a fork and a house—to increase the visual interest and provide a place for the viewer's eye to focus momentarily.

May We Be Your Force for Healing

Throughout history, people have, by their lives or actions, been forces for healing. The prime example of such an individual is Jesus. He demonstrated how we are to respect those in need of physical or emotional help. But Jesus didn't heal only the physical ailment. He healed sin-filled hearts with His sacrifice on the cross.

Because God is at work in our lives, He will help us address the physical, emotional, and spiritual needs we see. His love is reflected through us. We can be like Martin Luther King Jr. and find ways to excise and heal the deep scars of hatred. We can be like Mother Teresa and serve the unwanted and the unloved. We can be like former U.S. President Jimmy Carter and provide the poor with decent, affordable housing. Who will be God's force for healing? The teacher, the pastor, me, or …? No matter our position, we pray that God would use us to accomplish His healing work.

For this design, follow the "No-Pattern Method" on page 10. Use a single piece of cloth for the flower. Trace the lines of the petals directly onto the cloth. Use permanent felt-tip markers (noted on the design) to outline the parts of the flower, the stem, and the thorns. A thick line (3/16"–1/4") is best, depending on the size of the completed banner and its viewing distance.

BANNERS FOR SPECIFIC SITUATIONS

The following eight banners focus on specific situations that not every congregation or organization may encounter. These issues might be controversial or the images might be more graphic than those in the rest of this book. Consider using these banners for services with a special emphasis, such as Life Sunday. If your church is active in prison ministry, ministry with the disabled, or gang intervention, display the appropriate designs in meeting areas. Or if your church sponsors recovery groups, the groups could display the appropriate banners during meetings.

As with the other designs, these banners reflect God's call to take His message of love and reconciliation to the world. While these issues may be especially sensitive or controversial, Christians need to address them. The banners can be one way to invite discussion and encourage prayerful consideration about how God wants His people to address a given topic.

Treat Them as Your Brother and Sister

The stylized depiction of a person in a wheelchair appears in every parking lot and on many car license plates, building entrances, and in public rest rooms. It is one of the most recognized symbols in society. By law we accommodate the disabled, granting employment opportunities and greater access to public facilities, transit systems, and communications networks. But attitudes can't be legislated. Do you get angry about those prime parking spaces you can't use on a rainy day? Do you think, even for a moment, that people in wheelchairs aren't qualified for jobs?

How does your church enable those with special needs to participate? Do you have an elevator or access ramps? Are your rest rooms accessible? Can those with physical disabilities approach the altar? Do you provide large-print hymnals, worship bulletins, and Bibles? Do you announce special service instructions (for example, "Please be seated") rather than use only a hand motion? Can your confirmation, Sunday school, and day school teachers work with students with learning challenges? These are only a few of the questions Christians need to address—and I haven't even touched on our personal attitudes.

LETTERING (12)   BACKGROUND (17)

LETTERING (1)

14

14

14

7

7

BACKGROUND (17)

2

2

2

15

15

2

15

2

14

14

2

14

2

15

14

2

2

2

14

14

2

14

2

2

14

We Used to Be Two

This design was inspired by an author's use of Song of Songs 4:12 ("You are a garden locked up") as an analogy for her divorce recovery process. Divorce is a death … the death of a dream. As with any death, there is grief. The individual must work through rejection, loneliness, reduced income, and even a change of address, just to name a few issues. The newly divorced person often feels out of place around married friends. The individual feels "locked up," shut off from the resources to work through the negative emotions and move on.

But God offers this truth: Nothing is impossible with Him. Just as marriage joined two hearts into one, God will help those who are divorced learn to live as two independent people. He will be there as the grief is processed, the tough decisions made, the hurt feelings confronted. At the appropriate time, God will help turn the key and unlock the garden. He will encourage those who are divorced to blossom and grow into the beautiful creatures He has planned.

This banner could be used by a divorce recovery group within the church or in a special service that focuses on the causes and results of divorce in the Christian community.

Faith and Love Are Greater than Prison Bars

The hostages held in Lebanon by Muslim extremists were perhaps the most notable example of the triumph of faith and love over prison bars. Their imprisonment united this country in prayer as few events have before.

Behind the locked doors, Thomas Sutherland, Terry Anderson, and the others demonstrated the power of faith and love. Following his release, Terry Anderson witnessed to this power. He told one interviewer that a Bible was his most treasured book during his captivity. As he read and re-read Scripture, God changed his outlook on life. In fact, Anderson says that bitterness towards his captors has no place in his life now. He even prays for them.

We have experienced imprisonment—as Satan's hostages. But Jesus destroyed the chains that held us and threw wide the doors of our sin-filled prison. His death and resurrection won for us forgiveness of sins and life eternal with Him in heaven. We can, as Terry Anderson has, forgive those who harm us. We can pray for them because Jesus has set us free.

CHERISH AND PROTECT OUR HOME

LETTERING (12)

Cherish and Protect Our Home

Too often we fail to look at the whole earth as our home—a gift from our heavenly Father to pass on to future generations. Our sinful nature causes us to focus on the immediate gain, not the long-term loss. We tear the ground apart seeking minerals and ores, clear-cut forests for lumber and paper, and flood formerly inhabited canyons just to keep our lawns green. Scientists say we are driving species of plants and animals to extinction at a rate 1,000 times the pace of the prevailing rate since prehistory. We may be bulldozing or burning plants with the potential to cure unconquered diseases such as AIDS. How does this show wise stewardship of the world God created and entrusted to us?

Since Adam and Eve's fall, we have demonstrated a lack of respect for the world God made. We think the loss of one element won't harm the whole. But it does. Adam and Eve's one sin has affected every human and every segment of this world.

Only God could set things right. And He did when He sent Jesus to earth. Yes, we still mistreat His creation, but we have the promise of a new creation that nothing can destroy. As we share the world of nature with our children, we also share the world of faith.

Put an End to the Killing

Debates rage. Tempers flare. Lines are drawn. The hot topic? Abortion.

On one side, abortion-rights groups angrily demand greater protection for clinic workers and doctors who perform abortions. On the other side, pro-lifers display pictures of fetuses contorted in pain and block access to clinics.

One of the greatest ironies, though, is that some radical pro-life activists see nothing wrong with taking the life of a doctor who performs abortions. Such extremists claim this is "justifiable homicide" because it saves a baby's life. The immediate message of this design is to end abortion. Its larger message is that the killing must stop on both sides. Murder is never justified.

When the abortion issue arises, we must share God's message of Law and Gospel. He has commanded us not to kill. This command includes the unborn, the aged, the mentally disabled, the physically disabled. It also includes the doctors who perform abortions. But there is also Good News. Even if we have had an abortion, urged someone to have one, or performed one, we can ask God's forgiveness and receive it. Jesus has won that forgiveness for us on the cross. What a life-affirming message to share on both sides of the abortion line.

ALL LETTERING (2)

A PLAGUE

...that knows no class or racial boundaries

A Plague That Knows No Class or Racial Boundaries

America's drug epidemic is horrifying. Dealers serve up a smorgasbord of intoxicants—marijuana, heroin, crack, LSD, uppers, downers—to line their pockets. They have no regard for the suffering their products cause.

Those on the front lines of the drug war report that drug use has invaded all segments of society, from poor neighborhoods to suburbia to the farm belt. Across the United States, drug counselors report rising numbers of professionals—doctors, nurses, professors, executives, air-traffic controllers—trying to kick out-of-control habits.

Satan uses drugs to trick us into thinking we are in control of our lives. But there are consequences for sin. Stories abound of users injecting, pill-popping, and smoking their way through trust funds, savings accounts, and credit lines. After buying their way into addiction, they try to buy their way out by opting for "in" cures. They find there are no quick fixes.

God provides the only solution to addiction. It involves trust—trust that God is stronger than the need for another hit. Through Word and Sacrament this trust is strengthened as the Holy Spirit works in the believer's heart.

Guns and Attitudes: An Explosive Combination

While researching these banner themes, I came across three magazine articles that spoke eloquently about guns and violence. Each article showed that violence has become a way of life for our children. Kids view guns as a status symbol, a way to get respect, a source of power. They don't seem to grasp the serious consequences of carrying a weapon or using one. Our children have become callous. They believe that a gun solves every problem.

Violence is another manifestation of our sinfulness. Whether with fists or knives or guns, we seem to take pleasure in pain. We feel bigger, stronger, more important if we know others fear us.

Jesus didn't see the need to defeat Satan with muscle. When the devil came to tempt Him in the desert, Jesus defeated Him with words—God's words. And when it came time to complete His Father's plan for salvation, Jesus didn't arm His followers. He went quietly to the cross and offered Himself as the sacrifice. More powerful than any weapon, Jesus' death and resurrection destroyed Satan's power over us. We have forgiveness. We have the Holy Spirit working in us to move us past violence to words of peace.

LETTERING (2)

"Can't young people get together without slaughtering each other?"

UPPER AREA (5)

4
4
4
4

5
5
5
5

4
4

LOWER AREA (2)

Can't Young People Get Together without Slaughtering Each Other?

The caption for this design is one man's commentary on the growing menace of teen violence. As I read this question, I envisioned blood-stained pavement beneath my feet. This gruesome image seemed to convey the reckless disregard for human life exhibited by gangs.

This banner might have application in a school setting during a gang prevention emphasis. It might also be useful in a youth group setting when issues such as violence, prejudice, and peer pressure are discussed. Use it to launch discussions about how your church or school might become involved in gang intervention programs. Or it might lead to discussion of ways to keep kids off the streets and involved in nonviolent activities.